You Can Call Me Lizzy

By Jana Yankoviz Dalrymple

Illustrated by Cher Jiang & Wendy Wei

This is a work of nonfiction. No names have been changed, no characters invented, no events fabricated.

Illustrations by Cher Jiang & Wendy Wei
Book design by Laura Moreno

ISBN 979-8-218-34087-2

This book is dedicated to our sons Austin, Jackson, and Justin, and grandson Jayden, whose amazing dogs have shared many years of unconditional love, companionship, and entertainment!

I'm a yellow labrador retriever, and my human family got me on a warm summer day from a sweet lady who lived on a farm. My boy Jackson was six years old at the time, and I was eight weeks old. I had six puppy brothers and sisters and my boy picked me, the tiniest one, for his very own!

He searched in a baby names book for days before he decided to name me "Elizabeth," but you can call me "Lizzy."

After I said goodbye to my doggie mama and daddy and my puppy brothers and sisters, we started the long ride to my new home.

I was so happy to have a new family, a human mama and daddy, and two boys! I rode in the back seat with my boy and his older brother Austin. My boy Jackson sure was cute. He had dark hair and blue eyes. He held me close, and hugged and petted me all the way to my new home.

I knew he was the boy for me.

I felt so safe in his arms.

When we got there, I wasn't too sure about that great big place. It was so much bigger than my kennel and buildings at the farm where I had lived for weeks with my doggie family.

There was another doggie at my new house, a cocker spaniel, named "Snoopy," who belonged to Austin. Snoopy was a few years older than me and seemed very happy to meet me. During the day we would play with our boys in the workshop and out in the yard. At night we had special beds in that workshop. We had our very own bedroom. It was full of all kinds of things I had never seen before!

Just a couple days after I started living at my new home, I was playing with my doggie brother. I don't really know how it happened, but all of a sudden, my head was in his mouth! My boy came to my rescue and said,

"Snoopy, get Lizzy's head out of your mouth!"

I was a little scared, but he didn't hurt me and was only playing with me. Actually, he was getting to be an old doggie and I was probably pestering him. I honestly didn't mean to get him in trouble. I was just playing like I used to with my puppy family.

Soon after that we both learned how to "play nice."

I was really loving my new life and wanted to thank my family for all they did for me. I wanted to give them a gift!

I decided to carry plastic jars of nails and screws from the workshop to the back deck and give to them. I was pretty proud of myself, but Dad had a funny look on his face. He didn't scold me, but soon after that, those jars were put up on a high shelf in the workshop!

Hmmm, maybe that wasn't such a good idea after all.

The warm weather continued and the whole family, including Snoopy and me, enjoyed getting on our floating wooden dock and paddling around our little neighborhood lake.

It was such a fun time! It was so calm and peaceful.

I heard all kinds of birds singing and saw turtles sunning themselves on logs in the water. As we floated by, the neighbors waved to us from their backyards.

The first day out, Jackson got off the dock and into the lake onto a little swimming pool raft. I thought I needed to rescue him, so I jumped in the lake and swam over to him!

Snoopy was just fine to stay on the dock and watch it all happen. Silly me! Jackson didn't need rescued. He knew how to swim, and so did I. My family was sure surprised and so was I at how well I could swim my first time in the water! I was only ten weeks old at that time.

As the weeks passed I enjoyed swimming many more times with my family, while my doggie brother slept on the dock.

Another surprising adventure was when
I jumped into the lake and swam after
the ducks and geese. I would swim so fast
that they would have to fly away to keep
me from catching up to them! My family
was worried about me being able to swim
that far, but I was just fine. I would swim
back to them all by myself! I was always
surprising them with my swimming skills.

In no time at all, summer was over and Jackson and Austin went back to school. My mom went back to teaching, and my dad still went off to work each day.

One day, I got a really nice surprise and got to go to Jackson's classroom for Show and Tell. There were so many little girls and boys who wanted to pet and hug me. The kids loved me and I was so excited to spend time with them. I thought that maybe I would like to go to first grade, too! I stretched out on my tummy on the nice, cool floor.

I could stay there all day doing that!

Later in the school year, Snoopy and I thought we would go on some adventures to pass the time while they were gone.

Some days, when Snoopy wasn't too tired, we traveled down the road after everyone left. We saw all kinds of new things, new people, other doggies, and smelled lots of new smells. We always made it back before our family got home.

Those adventures continued for a while until one very sad day when I came home alone.

I guess that day's adventures were too much for old Snoopy. I could run much faster than him and didn't realize that he wasn't behind me as I ran home. My family found him lying peacefully on the side of the road, just as if he had gone to sleep, but my doggie brother had died.

We all loved him so much. I was so lonely without him. I spent more time in the house with my family and we comforted each other over the next few weeks. I hope that I helped them as much as they helped me!

Very soon after that, Dad built a great big pen next to the workshop. I could play safely in the pen, go in and out the doggie door, and stay cool on hot days and warm on cold days inside the workshop.

I really liked that.

Of course, I still got to play out in the open yard with Jackson, Austin, Mom, and Dad when they were outside with me.

KAPAUN
MEN

As I got older, I invented ways to make a game of almost anything. One day, Dad was cutting the stalks of bamboo that grew around the lake. He tossed them in a big trash pile and I thought I would help him. I grabbed them in my mouth and took them back to where he was cutting the other stalks. I could just about do that faster than he could cut them!

After all, I AM a retriever.

He got that same funny look on his face again, but then, smiled and patted me on the head. I guess I made him work twice as hard that day!

Another fun game for me was to take one of my toys that no longer had stuffing in it out in the open yard and roll all over it on my back. After that, I'd hold it in my mouth and spin in circles. Finally, I'd carry it over to the edge of the lake and toss it in. Of course, I'd jump in, swim over to it, and bring it back to the edge of the lake. I would do that over and over.

Talk about fun!

It was true about time flying by when you're having fun, because, before I knew it, I was going to be a doggie mama!

I wasn't too sure about that, but Mom said not to worry and that I would know how to take care of my puppies.

I started to get excited about that new part of my life! I would daydream about what they would look like and how many there would be.

Soon after that, Dad decided that he would get some ducks and geese from his cousin to keep on our property. My family brought them home in "Blue Boy," their old blue truck. Mom said not to let them out while I was out of the pen. Dad said that I wouldn't bother them since I was moving so slowly, because I was about ready to have my puppies!

Boy, did I fool them! I hopped into that truck bed and tried to play with the ducks and geese. I was barkin' and they were quackin' and honkin' and the truck was rockin'! They all flew off and we never saw them again!

Mom said, "I told you so!" Dad never brought any more ducks or geese home again!

Before long, I had eight puppies!

There were two girls and six boys. Every one of them was black. They were so cute and I knew that I would love being a mama.

One of the puppy girls, who my family named "Angel," was so tiny, and, even as a new doggie mama, I knew that she was sick. I was so sad when she didn't live through the first night. My family assured me that I did everything I could and said I was a really good mama.

I was so upset, but I knew I would take very good care of my seven puppies. They were just perfect and so full of energy. Some days, they wore me out!

It was hard work, but Mom was right. I DID know exactly how to take care of them!

When my puppies got a little older,
my family put different colored collars
on them to tell them apart. That was so
silly, I knew which one was which!

They took a picture of them in a
great big blue wheelbarrow. They were
having so much fun!

When they got big enough, it was
time for them to go and live with their
human families.

My family did keep one of the boys, for Austin. He named him "Hilton."

From the time he was just a few weeks old, he would howl when my family asked him to. Sometimes, they called him "Howling Hilton." All they had to do was say, "Howl, Hilton" and he would form an "o" with his little mouth and howl.

If my mom would sing in a real high voice, he would howl along with her!

Days turned into weeks.

Weeks turned into months.

Months turned into years.

My boy Hilton and I lived many happy years with our family. I was so grateful that Jackson picked me and that Austin picked Hilton! As we got older, my hearing wasn't so good and Hilton's eyesight wasn't either. So, we took really good care of each other.

After all, that's what puppy and human families do!